* Bring out the melody in the left hand in measures 14–17.

Silent Night
Andante (♩ = 92–100)
27
p
31
35
mp
39

43
mf
47
mp rit.
mf più mosso
Joy to the World
Maestoso (♩ = 92–108)
50
f
53

56
mf
60
mp
63
mf
f
67
meno mosso
ff
rit.